Date __5/10/09__
Mothers Day

Dear

ξ Mom - Rebecca Hockett "53"

_____

_____

_____

_____

_____

_____

From

Amber Sanders "23"

To Mom, with Love

Art and text © Karla Dornacher, licensed by Suzanne Cruise
Artwork and text licensed by J Countryman, used by permission.

© 2003 Christian Art Gifts, RSA
        Christian Art Gifts Inc., IL, USA

Designed by Christian Art Gifts

Printed in China

ISBN 978-1-86920-327-6

07 08 09 10 11 12 13 14 15 16 – 15 14 13 12 11 10 9 8 7 6

To Mom, with Love

Mom, you're a star

KARLA DORNACHER

christian
art gifts®

In everything
give thanks

BIRD
SEED

Her children arise
and call her blessed.

Proverbs 31:28

In everything
give thanks

Thank you, Mom, for putting our need
for love and kisses and hugs,
above the need for cleaning closets
and vacuuming the rugs!

I know there's something to be said
for keeping down the dust,
but where cleanliness is optional...
laughter is a must.

You kept our home neat and tidy,
the dishes were always done,
but we could always count on you
to play and have some fun.

So I'm grateful for you, Mom,
for teaching us what's best,
for showing us how to balance
work and play and rest.

You shine like stars in the universe, as you hold out the word of life.

Dear Mom,
You have been a shining
star in my life,
a beacon of hope, strong
and sure, a light to guide
me through
the storms of life.

Seeing the Light
of Christ in you,
has given me
an example to follow
and because of you
the love of God
is a reality in my life.

You light up my life!

A mother sows seeds of love and care,
she nurtures them with hugs and prayer.
With patience and discipline she weeds,
she waters with wisdom and kind deeds.

And the labor of love she so richly invests,
will bring her a harvest of blessedness.

I tasted of God's goodness
through all my childhood days,
the sweetness of His nature,
in so many different ways.

I tasted of His sunshine,
through my mother's smile.
I tasted of His patience,
as she endured through every trial.

I tasted of His tenderness,
as she comforted my fears.
I tasted His compassion,
as she wiped away my tears.

To my Family with love

Sweet Words

Peachy Praise

Charity Chutney

to Friends

Prayer Preserves

Taste and see

that the Lord is good

I tasted God's great blessing,
a gift from heaven above.
I had a taste of God's own heart,
through my mother's love.

13

In everything give thanks

Dear Mom,

God created you in His image and you are precious in His sight. He knew you before you were even born and placed within you a mother's heart. He knew the day would come for me to be born and in His great grace, He wanted me to have you as my mom and you to have me as your child.

I am grateful that He chose to place me in your arms, for He knew you would hold me with affection, discipline me with love, and encourage me to be the person He designed me to be.

It is no accident I was born
to you and I am eternally
thankful that by His
divine design I am privileged
to call you my mother.

My Mom...

She is clothed with strength and dignity;
she can laugh at days to come.
She speaks with wisdom,
and faithful instruction is on her tongue.
She watches over the affairs of her household
and does not eat the bread of idleness.
Her children arise and call her blessed;
her husband also, and he praises her.

"Many women do noble things,
but you surpass them all."

Charm is deceptive, and beauty is
fleeting; but a woman who fears the LORD
is to be praised. Give her the reward
she has earned, and let her works
bring her praise at the city gate.

Proverbs 31:29~31

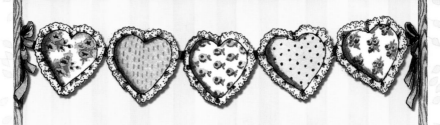

A house is just a building,
four walls and a roof above,
but you, dear Mom,
transformed our house
to a home filled
with laughter and love.

Your wisdom and compassion,
understanding beyond measure,
filled every room
of our hearts and home
with the most rare
and beautiful treasure.

18

By wisdom
a house is built,
and through
understanding
it is established;
through knowledge
its rooms are filled
with rare and
beautiful treasures.
Proverbs 24:3~4

I know that being a mom isn't easy,
you don't have time to ever be bored.
But be encouraged to make it a habit
to spend some daily time with the Lord.

His Word will be like food to your soul,
His Spirit will quench your thirst.
He's promised to give you all you need
if only you'll put Him first.

Whoever is thirsty, let him come;
and whoever wishes, let him take
the free gift of the water of life.

Revelation 22:17

In everything give thanks

Children are
a heritage
from
the LORD.

Psalm 127:3, NKJV

With great confidence, God placed
my life into your hands.
I know I arrived as a small bundle
of blessing ~ a gift of life
given to bring you great joy ~
but I know it hasn't always been
easy as we've had to grow together ~
discovering God's plan and
purpose for bringing me into
your life ... and into this world.

Thank you, Mom, for being
the instrument God used
to mold and shape my character,
while still allowing me to be
the person He created me to be.

A bouquet of blessings
just for you!
Thank you, Mom,
for all you do!

The LORD bless you
and keep you;
The LORD make His face
shine upon you
and be gracious to you;
The LORD turn His face toward
you and give you peace.
Numbers 6:24~26

Finally, brethren,
whatever things are true,
whatever things are noble,
whatever things are just,
whatever things are pure,
whatever things are lovely,
whatever things are
of good report,
if there is any virtue and if
there is anything praiseworthy ~
meditate on these things.

Philippians 4:8, NKJV

Thinking of you
makes me smile!

Dear Mom,

I know you sacrificed a lot as my mother ~

You gave up your sleep so I could rest in your arms.

You gave up your own dreams so I could fulfill mine.

You gave up your time so I would know you care.

You gave up your own needs so you could provide for me.

Lord, bless my mom ~ for the sacrifices of her love.

Give, and it will be given to you.
A good measure, pressed down,
shaken together and running over,
will be poured into your lap.
For with the measure you
use, it will be measured to you.

Luke 6:38

28

As a mother comforts her child, so will I comfort you.

Isaiah 66:13

29

Thanks be to God

for His indescribable gift!
2 Corinthians 9:15

Dear Mom,

There are no words to express how much I love you. I could write a million poems, send a field of flowers or give you a stand~ing ovation, but still you could not know the depth of my love or the gratefulness of my heart for having you as my mom.

Thank you for loving me.

In everything
give thanks

Thank you, Lord, for memories
of sunshine smiles and laughter,
for butterfly kisses
and hugs of joy
that will last forever after.

Dear Lord,
   Bless my mom for the care
she took to build memories
that have been and will be a
foundation of faith, love and
joy for me all the days of my
life.

THE MEMORY
OF THE
RIGHTEOUS
WILL BE
A BLESSING.

Proverbs 10:7

33

Be hospitable to one another. . .

1 Peter 4:9, NKJV

God calls us to be hospitable
to one another without grumbling.
He asks us to use our gifts
and abilities to bless one another,
bringing glory to His Name.

Mother, I appreciate
the example you have been to me.
You not only believe God's Word,
you live it, and I just know the angels
in heaven are standing in line,
taking numbers, longing to be
entertained by your gift of hospitality!

God is truly glorified in your life!

Do not forget to entertain
strangers, for by so doing some have
unwittingly entertained angels.

Hebrews 13:2, NKJV

You stand alone
among all others,
as the most beautiful
and caring mother.

Karla Dornacher.

Thank you, Mom,
you are the heart of our home ~
a high calling and valued position.
Your role is one of influence,
of honor and tradition.

You allow God's love
to fill the rooms of your heart,
overflowing with kindness and care,
you warm our home and touch
the lives of all who enter there.

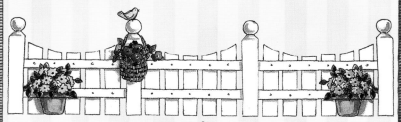

As for me and my house, we will serve the LORD.

Joshua 24:15, NKJV

Just as God opens His heart
and puts out His welcome sign for all,
beckoning us to come into His presence,
you always opened
our home and your heart
to all those who knocked at the door ~
family, friends, neighbors
and even those you did not know.

Mom, thank you for teaching me
that the true meaning
of hospitality is an open invitation
and a welcome mat that knows no stranger,
nor turns away anyone in need of a friend.

Fond family memories
and a cozy glowing fire ~
both delight the heart
and warm the home.

Your love, Mother, was
always the spark that
kept the fire burning!

Now godliness with
contentment is great gain.

1 Timothy 6:6, NKJV

Contentment is an attitude,
like a treasured piece of art,
its beauty and value are priceless
when it's framed with a godly heart.

Thank you, Mom ~ for decorating our
home with the joy of true contentment.

For the eyes of the LORD
run to and fro
throughout the whole earth,
to show Himself strong
on behalf of those
whose heart is loyal to Him.

2 Chronicles 16:9, NKJV

Thank you, Lord,
for giving me a mother whose
heart has been loyal to You.

Through her life,
I have known Your love,
Your comfort, Your wisdom,
and Your ways.

Reveal Yourself to her, Lord,
in a special way today ...
and bless her heart!